EXPLORING THE STATES

North Carolina

THE TAR HEEL STATE

by Davy Sweazey

BELLWETHER MEDIA • MINNEAPOLIS, MN

Note to Librarians, Teachers, and Parents:

Blastoff! Readers are carefully developed by literacy experts and combine standards-based content with developmentally appropriate text.

Level 1 provides the most support through repetition of high-frequency words, light text, predictable sentence patterns, and strong visual support.

Level 2 offers early readers a bit more challenge through varied simple sentences, increased text load, and less repetition of high-frequency words.

Level 3 advances early-fluent readers toward fluency through increased text and concept load, less reliance on visuals, longer sentences, and more literary language.

Level 4 builds reading stamina by providing more text per page, increased use of punctuation, greater variation in sentence patterns, and increasingly challenging vocabulary.

Level 5 encourages children to move from "learning to read" to "reading to learn" by providing even more text, varied writing styles, and less familiar topics.

Whichever book is right for your reader, Blastoff! Readers are the perfect books to build confidence and encourage a love of reading that will last a lifetime!

This edition first published in 2014 by Bellwether Media, Inc.

No part of this publication may be reproduced in whole or in part without written permission of the publisher. For information regarding permission, write to Bellwether Media, Inc., Attention: Permissions Department, 5357 Penn Avenue South, Minneapolis, MN 55419.

Library of Congress Cataloging-in-Publication Data

Sweazey, Davy.
  North Carolina / by Davy Sweazey.
    pages cm. – (Blastoff! readers. Exploring the states)
  Includes bibliographical references and index.
  Summary: "Developed by literacy experts for students in grades three through seven, this book introduces young readers to the geography and culture of North Carolina"–Provided by publisher.
  ISBN 978-1-62617-032-2 (hardcover : alk. paper)
  1. North Carolina–Juvenile literature. I. Title.
  F254.3.S94 2014
  975.6–dc23

                                                                    2013008934

Table of Contents

Where Is North Carolina?

Tennessee

Greensboro ●

Great Smoky
Mountains
National Park ←

Charlotte
●

Georgia

South
Carolina

North Carolina covers 52,663 square miles (136,397 square kilometers) in the southeastern United States. The state nestles between Virginia to the north and South Carolina to the south. Its southwest corner touches Tennessee and Georgia. The Appalachian Mountains rise where these three states meet.

Virginia

N
W · E
S

· Durham

★ Raleigh

North Carolina

↖ Cape Hatteras

Atlantic Ocean

Did you know?
Many ships wrecked near Cape Hatteras. It is called the "Graveyard of the Atlantic."

North Carolina is one of fourteen states that border the Atlantic Ocean. It extends farthest into the ocean at **Cape** Hatteras. The capital city of Raleigh lies near the center of North Carolina. Raleigh is the second largest city in the state.

History

The Cherokee, Catawba, and other **Native** Americans were the first to live in the region now called North Carolina. The first European settlers arrived in 1585. North Carolina was one of the original thirteen **colonies** that declared independence from Great Britain. It became the twelfth state in 1789. North Carolina joined the **Confederacy** during the **Civil War**.

fun fact

Early settlers from Great Britain landed on Roanoke Island in North Carolina. They all mysteriously disappeared within several years. Historians call their settlement the Lost Colony.

North Carolina Timeline!

1524: Giovanni da Verrazzano is the first European to travel to North Carolina.

1650: Settlers establish the first permanent European colony near Albermarle Sound.

1729: The Carolina Colony separates into North Carolina and South Carolina.

1776: North Carolina declares independence from Great Britain.

1789: North Carolina becomes the twelfth state.

1830: The U.S. government passes the Indian Removal Act. The act forces Native Americans to leave their homes and move west.

1861: North Carolina enters the Civil War to fight for the Confederacy.

1903: The Wright brothers successfully fly the first powered airplane at Kitty Hawk.

1960: Four young African-American men protest racial separation in the Greensboro sit-ins.

Greensboro sit-ins

Giovanni da Verrazzano

Wright brothers

The Land

North Carolina's landscape slopes from mountains in the west toward the ocean in the east. Appalachian mountain ranges such as the Blue Ridge and Great Smoky accent the western border. At 6,684 feet (2,037 meters), Mount Mitchell is the tallest mountain east of the Mississippi River.

Rolling hills in the Piedmont **Plateau** stretch east from the mountains. Sand **dunes**, swamps, and beaches dot the flat Coastal **Plain** along the ocean. **Barrier islands** called the Outer Banks shelter the mainland coast from large waves.

fun fact !

Old stories tell of pirate treasure buried on the sandy islands of the Outer Banks.

North Carolina's Climate

average °F

spring
Low: 51°
High: 70°

summer
Low: 67°
High: 86°

fall
Low: 52°
High: 72°

winter
Low: 34°
High: 53°

Outer Banks

Great Smoky Mountains

The Great Smoky Mountains rise in western North Carolina and stretch into Tennessee. The mountains make up part of the Appalachians. A misty blue appearance earned the Great Smokies their name.

Abundant rain fills rivers and streams in the Smokies. Many of the streams tumble over waterfalls. Plants thrive in the wet, **humid** environment. Orchids, violets, and other wildflowers bloom in the spring. The thick blanket of trees turns orange, yellow, and brown in autumn. National forests and the Great Smoky Mountains National Park attract many **tourists**.

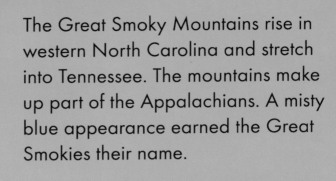

fun fact

The Great Smokies are called the "Salamander Capital of the World." Thirty different kinds of salamanders live there!

fun fact !

The Venus flytrap is a plant native to southeastern North Carolina. The flytrap catches and eats insects and other tiny animals!

Black bears roam among the forests of North Carolina. Beavers and otters play in the rivers and streams. Trout, bass, and sunfish glide through the water below them. Cottonmouths and other **venomous** snakes lurk in the Great Dismal Swamp.

Venus flytrap

mockingbird

otter

cottonmouth

Rabbits, skunks, and opossums scurry through dogwood and rhododendron plants. Cardinals, woodpeckers, and mockingbirds sing from the trees. Past the coastal palm trees, dolphinfish, marlin, and other saltwater fish swim in the ocean.

Landmarks

People know North Carolina for its beauty. Visitors travel the Blue Ridge Parkway to see the majestic view from the mountaintops. The tallest lighthouse in the U.S. stands on the Cape Hatteras National Seashore. It used to guide ships in the dangerous Atlantic waters. Today, it greets visitors.

The Fort Raleigh National Historic Site tells the story of the Roanoke settlers. The history of flight is celebrated at the Wright Brothers National Memorial. In 1903, the Wright brothers launched the first powered airplane flight from Kitty Hawk.

Wright Brothers National Memorial

fun fact

The city of High Point claims to have the world's largest chest of drawers. The special piece of furniture stands 38 feet (12 meters) tall!

Cape Hatteras
Lighthouse

Charlotte

Charlotte is the largest city in North Carolina. It lies in the center of the state near the border of South Carolina. A rich colonial history gives the city its **character**.

In 1799, Charlotte experienced the first American gold rush. The U.S. **Mint** in Charlotte turned the gold into coins. The Mint is now an art museum. However, the city still ranks as one of the largest banking centers in the country. Charlotte also holds a great number of attractions to explore. They include the Charlotte Nature Museum and a children's museum called Discovery Place.

NASCAR Hall of Fame

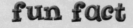

! **fun fact**
NASCAR stands for National Association for Stock Car Auto Racing. Charlotte is home to the NASCAR Hall of Fame.

Working

Most North Carolinians have **service jobs**. Many researchers and scientists work in a large complex called Research Triangle Park in the Durham area. Large universities, banks, and military bases offer jobs across the state. Tourism provides work at hotels, museums, and restaurants.

North Carolina leads other states in **manufacturing**. Workers carefully make food products, chemicals, and medicine. People work for airlines and trucking companies to transport goods. Some North Carolinians continue to farm. Most of them raise chickens, pigs, sweet potatoes, or tobacco. Some people work as miners or fishers.

Where People Work in North Carolina

manufacturing
10%

farming and
natural resources
2%

government
15%

services
73%

stock car racing

North Carolinians are proud of their sports teams. The University of North Carolina Tar Heels and the Duke University Blue Devils inspire basketball lovers. Hockey fans cheer for the Carolina Hurricanes in Raleigh. The Carolina Panthers entertain football supporters in Charlotte.

North Carolina's mild climate is perfect for outdoor activities. Hikers and skiers play in the mountains. The ocean invites visitors to swim, windsurf, and fish. Green courses attract golfers from around the world. Stock car racing started in North Carolina and is the official state sport.

Hush Puppies

Ingredients:

1/2 cup flour

1/2 cup yellow cornmeal

1/2 teaspoon salt

1/4 teaspoon baking soda

1/2 teaspoon black pepper

1 large egg

1/2 cup buttermilk

1/4 cup minced onion

2 cups vegetable oil for frying

Directions:

1. Combine the first five ingredients in a bowl.

2. Stir together egg and buttermilk. Add to dry ingredients, and stir until just moistened. Then stir in onion.

4. Pour oil in a large, heavy frying pan. Heat to 375°F.

5. Carefully drop batter by tablespoonfuls into oil. Fry in small batches for 3 minutes on each side, or until golden.

6. Drain on paper towels and serve immediately.

steamed clams

fun fact

In 1937, Vernon Rudolph started the Krispy Kreme doughnut company in Winston-Salem.

Seafood is popular in North Carolina. People near the coast enjoy crab and shrimp. They also eat tuna, flounder, and other fish. A plate of seafood in North Carolina is only complete with hush puppies. These treats are deep-fried corn cakes that often include onions.

Clambakes are a **tradition** learned from Native Americans who lived in the area. A clambake involves steaming clams and vegetables over hot stones in a pit. Hunters eat deer, geese, and other wild **game**. Barbecued pork is also a favorite of many North Carolinians.

Festival of Flowers

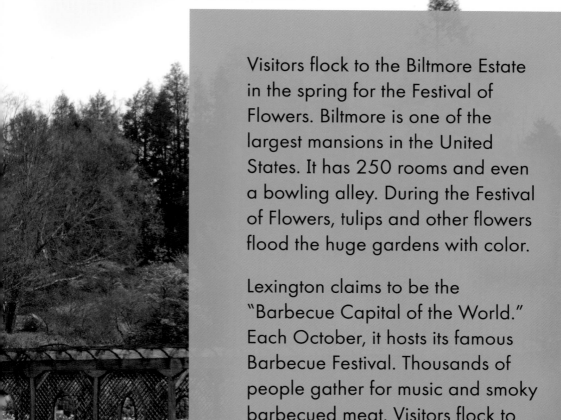

Visitors flock to the Biltmore Estate in the spring for the Festival of Flowers. Biltmore is one of the largest mansions in the United States. It has 250 rooms and even a bowling alley. During the Festival of Flowers, tulips and other flowers flood the huge gardens with color.

Lexington claims to be the "Barbecue Capital of the World." Each October, it hosts its famous Barbecue Festival. Thousands of people gather for music and smoky barbecued meat. Visitors flock to Benson each summer for Mule Days. A parade, **rodeos**, and mule contests entertain the crowd.

fun fact

Every fall, the Woolly Worm Festival takes place in Banner Elk. Families cheer for their caterpillar to win a race!

Bluegrass Music

Bluegrass music has been part of North Carolina culture since the 1940s. Its roots go back even further to the mountain music of the Appalachians. Bluegrass is a type of country music related to jazz and blues. Musicians play stringed instruments such as banjos, **mandolins**, and fiddles. Sometimes singers add **harmonies**.

Did you know?
North Carolinian Earl Scruggs became famous for his style of banjo picking. He used three fingers for picking at the strings.

Many events celebrate the tradition of bluegrass in North Carolina. MerleFest brings thousands of music fans to Wilkesboro each summer. The Blue Ridge Music Trails invite travelers to stop at musical locations along the Blue Ridge Parkway. Each stop offers a unique taste of the mountain music of North Carolina.

Fast Facts About North Carolina

North Carolina's Flag

North Carolina's flag has a blue band on the left side. The right side is red on top and white on the bottom. The initials NC, a star, and two ribbons are pictured in the blue band. "May 20th, 1775" is written on the top ribbon. "April 12th, 1776" is written on the bottom ribbon. Both dates represent North Carolina declaring independence from Great Britain.

State Flower
flowering dogwood

State Nicknames:	The Tar Heel State The Old North State
State Motto:	*Esse Quam Videri*; "To Be, Rather Than To Seem"
Year of Statehood:	1789
Capital City:	Raleigh
Other Major Cities:	Charlotte, Greensboro, Durham
Population:	9,535,483 (2010)
Area:	52,663 square miles (136,397 square kilometers); North Carolina is the 28th largest state.
Major Industries:	farming, services, research and technology, manufacturing
Natural Resources:	wood, soil, water, phosphate rock, granite, limestone
State Government:	120 representatives; 50 senators
Federal Government:	13 representatives; 2 senators
Electoral Votes:	15

State Bird
northern cardinal

State Animal
gray squirrel

Glossary

barrier islands—narrow, sandy islands that run next to a mainland coast

cape—a piece of land that sticks out into the water

character—unique nature

Civil War—a war between the northern (Union) and southern (Confederate) states that lasted from 1861 to 1865

colonies—territories settled and ruled by people from another country

Confederacy—the group of southern states in America that formed a new country in 1860; they fought against the northern states during the Civil War

dunes—hills of sand formed by wind

game—wild animals hunted for food or sport

harmonies—combinations of musical notes or chords that are pleasing to the ear

humid—hot and sticky

mandolins—pear-shaped stringed instruments

manufacturing—a field of work in which people use machines to make products

mint—a place where money is produced

native—originally from a specific place

plain—a large area of flat land

plateau—an area of flat, raised land

rodeos—events where people compete at tasks such as bull riding and calf roping; cowboys once completed these tasks as part of their daily work.

service jobs—jobs that perform tasks for people or businesses

tourists—people who travel to visit another place

tradition—a custom, idea, or belief handed down from one generation to the next

venomous—producing a poison that can harm or kill

To Learn More

AT THE LIBRARY

Prentzas, G. S. *Roanoke: The Lost Colony*. New York, N.Y.: Chelsea House, 2011.

Roberts, Angela. *NASCAR's Greatest Drivers*. New York, N.Y.: Random House, 2009.

Venezia, Mike. *The Wright Brothers: Inventors Whose Ideas Really Took Flight*. New York, N.Y.: Children's Press, 2010.

ON THE WEB

Learning more about North Carolina is as easy as 1, 2, 3.

1. Go to www.factsurfer.com.

2. Enter "North Carolina" into the search box.

3. Click the "Surf" button and you will see a list of related Web sites.

With factsurfer.com, finding more information is just a click away.

Index

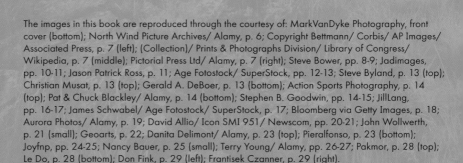